MALE SPORTS STARS

IN THIS SERIES

Superstars of Men's Figure Skating

Superstars of Men's Pro Wrestling

Superstars of Men's Soccer

Superstars of Men's Swimming and Diving

Superstars of Men's Tennis

Superstars of Men's Track and Field

MALE SPORTS STARS

Superstars of Men's SWIMMING AND DIVING

by Paula Edelson

CHELSEA HOUSE PUBLISHERS

Philadelphia

Picture Researcher: Joseph W. Wagner
Typography by Type Shoppe II Productions, Ltd.
Cover Illustrator: Bill Vann
Frontispiece Illustration: Steve Stroud

© 1999 by Chelsea House Publishers,
a division of Main Line Book Co.
Printed and bound in the United States of America.

First Printing

1 3 5 7 9 8 6 4 2

Library of Congress Cataloging-in-Publication Data applied for

ISBN 0-7910-4589-7

CONTENTS

CHAPTER 1
The Early Days 7

CHAPTER 2
Heroes of the Waves 17

CHAPTER 3
All About Mark 25

CHAPTER 4
The Americans Dominate 33

CHAPTER 5
The Greatest of Ease 45

CHAPTER 6
The Greatest of Them All 53

Chronology 62

Further Reading 63

Index 64

1 THE EARLY DAYS

For many of us, swimming is an activity of leisure, a great way to stay cool during the summer; for others, it is a marvelous exercise, perhaps the best workout people can get. Then there are those who swim competitively and spend hours every day in the water, swimming lap after lap for the sole purpose of winning a race. For these athletes, swimming is a labor of love. It is not a sport that has a professional league, or whose stars go on to become multimedia celebrities. Whereas basketball, football, and baseball make millionaires out of their best players, the finest swimmers can only hope and dream for a shot to compete in the Olympic Games, the highest competition for amateur athletes. Olympic champions are celebrated for being the finest athletes in a given sport, but their victories are not rewarded with money.

Today, of course, there are endorsement opportunities for champion swimmers, but that was not always the case. When swimming first became an Olympic sport in 1896, the first champion of the water, Alfred Hajos, did not make a dime from his athletic talent, but prospered in another, more sedentary, profession. Hajos won another Olympic medal 28 years later, this time as an architect who received a silver medal for his stadium architecture at the 1924 Paris games.

Alfred Hajos, Hungarian swimming champion at the 1896 Olympics, with some of his swimming medals.

Hajos won his Olympic titles—in the 100-meter and 1200-meter freestyle races—at what was the first modern Olympic Games in Athens, Greece, in 1896. That year, swimming was an event that featured four competitive races: the 400-, 1500-, and 100-meters, and a 200-meter race in which only sailors were allowed to compete.

At the 1996 games in Atlanta, a full century after Hajos' victories, the number of swimming events had expanded to a total of 16 individual and team races. The 100-year interval between the Athens and Atlanta games bore witness to a host of swimmers who left their marks on the sport—and on the world—through their mastery of what is one of the most grueling and demanding of athletic endeavors.

COMPETITIVE SWIMMING STROKES

There are four major strokes in competitive swimming. The first of these is the crawl, characterized by alternate overhead motion of the arms and strong, straight kicking of the legs and feet. Swimmers performing the crawl lie on their stomachs, face down in the water, and turn their heads to the side for air every three or four strokes. The crawl is the fastest of the strokes and is always chosen by competitors racing in the freestyle events, which allow swimmers to choose any stroke they wish.

The second stroke is the backstroke and features the same motions as the crawl except instead of lying face down in the water, the swimmer lies on his or her back. Backstroke is the only event in which swimmers remain in the water from start to finish. All other races begin with the competitor at poolside, ready to dive in when the starting gun sounds.

The third, the breaststroke, looks easy to many beginning swimmers but is extremely difficult. Face down, swimmers must push their hands straight forward from the breast, keep them under the surface of the water for the entire motion, then propel their arms, keeping them straight, back toward their bodies. In the meantime, their legs are thrust first up toward their bodies, knees bent, then straight out to each side, and finally together in what is known as a "frog," or breaststroke, kick.

The fourth stroke, the butterfly, is the newest and became an Olympic event in the 1956 Melbourne games. It is probably the most physically demanding and requires simultaneous overhead motion of the arms, along with a quick, powerful downward kick of the legs (the "dolphin" stroke).

Competitive swimming features events for each individual stroke. Most swimmers specialize in one or two of these strokes. Mark Spitz, for example, swam only the butterfly and freestyle events at the 1972 Olympics. The freestyle events include sprints (50 meters, 100 meters, and 200 meters), middle-distance (400 meters), and long-distance (1500 meters) races. The other strokes are raced at distances of 100 meters and 200 meters.

In addition to races that feature individual strokes are "medley" events in which competitors swim each stroke for a distance of 50 or 100 meters each. Another event called the "medley relay" features teams of four swimmers each who perform the different strokes in alternation in 50- or 100-meter legs.

THE HISTORY OF SWIMMING

Swimming as a sport dates back some 2,000 years to when water races were held in Japan. And before that, leisurely swimming was a popular pastime. There are stories about swimming in both the Bible and ancient Greek mythology. In fact, swimming was held in such high regard in the ancient world that the Greek philosopher Plato wrote that anyone who could not swim was simply not educated. Ancient and medieval figures known for their prowess in the water included Julius Caesar, Alexander the Great, and Charlemagne.

The first recorded swimming race occurred between two Americans who traveled to London in 1844 to compete in an event sponsored by the British National Swimming Society. These two racers first introduced the crawl stroke to the English, whose prior swimming repertoire included only the breaststroke. Thirty-one years later, the breaststroke was the stroke of choice of Captain Matthew Webb, who became the first person to swim the English Channel in 1875. One year later, Frederick Cavill, an Englishman living in Australia, demonstrated a leg kick he had seen natives use during his travels to the South Seas. The kick provided additional power to the crawl stroke and became known as the "Australian crawl." It is the same stroke used in freestyle competitions today.

When the first Olympic games were held in Athens in 1896, they featured only four swimming events, and eighteen swimmers from six countries vied for Olympic gold. Ten years later, the Federation Internationale de Natation Amateur (FINA) was formed at the 1908

London games to diversify and popularize the sport. Today, swimming remains one of the most elite and glamorous of all Olympic sports because of the efforts of FINA and the charisma of some of the early swimming champions.

DUKE KAHANAMOKU

One of these champions was Duke Paoa Kahinu Makoe Hulikohoa Kahanamoku who was born in Honolulu on August 24, 1890. He participated in five different Olympic games and won a total of five medals.

His reign began in 1911 when the 21-year-old Kahanamoku broke the record for the 100-meter freestyle by almost five seconds. One year later, he won two medals at the Stockholm games: a gold in the 100-meter freestyle and a silver in the 200-meter freestyle relay. During his qualifying heat in the 100-meter freestyle, Kahanamoku equaled the new world record that had been set earlier that year by Germany's Kurt Buetting. During the finals, however, he was so far ahead of the rest of the

The Duke churns the water again. Here, Duke Kahanamoku, the great Hawaiian freestyle swimmer, is pictured while training for a comeback in Los Angeles, CA.

field that he eased up at the halfway mark and still won the race by several lengths.

World War I forced cancellation of the 1916 Olympic Games and Kahanamoku had to wait until 1920 to defend his 100-meter freestyle gold medal. He did so by setting a new world record in the final, which took place on his 20th birthday.

Most swimmers are close to retirement by the time they hit the age of 30, but Kahanamoku's career was far from over. He won a silver in the 100-meter freestyle at the 1924 games, made the Olympic swim team as an alternate in 1928, and in 1932, 20 years after his first Olympics, served as an alternate on the U.S. Olympic water polo team. When Kahanamoku died in 1968, he had left his mark not only on virtually every water sport (he was one of the forefathers of the sport of surfing and played a major role in introducing it to the rest of the world) but also on Hollywood's silver screen, where he usually appeared as a Hawaiian king.

Kahanamoku may have been the first swimming champion to become a movie star, but he was not the last. Two other gold medalists from Kahanamoku's era went on to become Hollywood legends. The first of these was a German-born swimmer named Johnny Weismuller.

JOHNNY WEISMULLER

When Johnny Weismuller was born on June 2, 1904, doctors feared that he was suffering from a heart disorder that would leave him permanently weak and disabled. Nothing, however, was further from the truth for the

man who set swimming records in the water and swung tirelessly from tree to tree on the silver screen.

At the age of 18, Weismuller stunned the swimming world by becoming the first man to swim the 100-meter freestyle in less than a minute. Two years later, at the 1924 Olympics in Paris, Weismuller set an Olympic record by swimming that event in 59 seconds flat. Weismuller's time was more than 2 seconds faster than the second-place finisher, Duke Kahanamoku. Before the race began, Weismuller nervously glanced at his competitors and found that he was set to race in between two Kahanamokus: Duke and his brother, Sam. Sensing Weismuller's unease, the older Kahanamoku told him, "Johnny, good luck. The most important thing in this race is to get the American flag up there three times. Let's do it." And do it they did as Sam Kahanamoku's third-place finish sealed an American sweep of the event.

Johnny Weismuller, photographed at a practice session, shows his unique swimming style.

Johnny Weismuller won a total of four medals in the 1924 Olympics: golds in the 100- and 400-meter individual races and the 4 x 200 freestyle relay, and a bronze in water polo. Four years later in Amsterdam, he added two more medals: golds, once again in the 100-meter freestyle (breaking his own Olympic record by swimming the race in 58.6 seconds) and in the 4 x 200 freestyle relay. In addition to his sheer speed and power, Weismuller distinguished himself by swimming in what was then a completely unique fashion. He rode high in the water and would alternate sides when he came up to breathe so that he always knew where his opponents were. They were invariably behind him. In his 10-year career as an amateur swimmer, Weismuller was never defeated in distances between 50 yards and half a mile. During that time, he held 52 U.S. titles and 28 world records.

In 1932, four years after his final Olympic victory, Weismuller began his second career as Tarzan in *Tarzan the Ape Man*. He died in 1984 at the age of 80 and is probably remembered more for his performances on screen than for his prowess in the water.

Another swimmer turned movie star was Clarence "Buster" Crabbe.

BUSTER CRABBE

In 1932, the Olympics were held in Los Angeles. Spoiled by eight years of American dominance, the spectators were disappointed by the American men's lackluster performances. But all that changed in a flash. At the finals of the men's 400-meter freestyle, the crowd (Weismuller, now a movie star, among them) was set to cheer on a local boy. Crabbe was not only an American, but also a native Californian. Born in Los Angeles in 1909, he had won an Olympic bronze medal in the 1500-meter race at the 1928 Amsterdam games, but four years later desperately wanted a gold. The competition in the 400-meter freestyle event was fierce. Japanese swimmer Takahi Yokoyama had set Olympic records in the semifinal of the event and Jean Taris of France held the world record.

From the beginning, it was a two-man race. Taris grabbed the early lead and at the halfway mark held a comfortable two-and-one-half length lead. But in the second half of the race, Crabbe crept closer and closer as the crowd roared its support. At the 350-meter mark, the two men were dead even with one leg to go. Both swimmers sprinted head down for the edge of the pool. Everyone in the stadium—swimmers, ushers, and spectators—jumped up and down in excitement. Touching first by mere inches was Crabbe. He had beaten Taris by a tenth of a second.

"That tenth of a second," Crabbe later recalled, "completely changed my life." It was all Crabbe needed to ensure his place in Olympic history and in Hollywood. He would never win another Olympic medal, but his future was just as golden. Crabbe followed Weismuller from Olympic glory to film stardom, playing Tarzan in several films and gaining a cult following for his portrayals of Buck Rogers and Flash Gordon on the screen. He died at the age of 75 in 1983, one year before Johnny Weismuller.

Buster Crabbe in a publicity movie still.

2 HEROES OF THE WAVES

Buster Crabbe made a big splash at the 1932 Los Angeles Olympics, not only because he was a local boy who was a worthy successor to Johnny Weismuller, but also because he was the only American man to win a gold medal in swimming at those games. The other five top-place finishers in the six swimming events of that year were all from Japan, a water-bound nation that produced more than its share of powerful swimmers back in the 1930s. Their athletes were impressive because of their talents in the water and for their sheer youthfulness: three of the five Japanese medalists were still in high school.

One of these wonderboys who succeeded Weismuller as victor of the 100-meter freestyle race was a 15-year-old named Yasuji Mayazaki. Miyazaki brought his books with him to Los Angeles so that he wouldn't fall too far behind in his schooling. In between study sessions, Miyazaki managed to beat Weismuller's Olympic record time by .2 seconds and recorded a time of 58.0 in the semifinals.

In addition to the races won by Miyazaki and Kusuo Kitamura, Japan swept the 100-meter backstroke as Mesaji Kiyokawa, Toshio Irie, and Kentaro Kawatsu took first-, second- and third-place honors, respectively. And in the 200-meter breaststroke, Yoshiyuki Tsurata successfully defended his 1928 crown by beating fellow countryman Reizo Koike to grab the gold.

In the 1500-meter freestyle at the 1932 Los Angeles Olympics, Japanese swimmer K. Kitamura (right) won the gold and his teammate S. Makino (left) won the silver.

Yasoji Miyazaki of Japan won the gold medal in the 100-meter men's freestyle at the 1932 Olympics.

HITLER'S GAMES

Four years later, the Olympics were held in Berlin, Germany. In many ways, this was the most controversial of any Olympic contest. Adolph Hitler had seized control of Germany and the host country was about a year away from initiating what would be the most devastating war in European history.

Many Americans remember the 1936 games for Jesse Owens' one-man assault on the blonde, blue-eyed athletes from the host nation, which resulted in the American athelete's winning four gold medals in the men's track-and-field events.

The Germans were also outclassed in the water, this time not by an African American but by swimmers from Japan, the same country that had dominated the games four years before. Japanese swimmers won three individual golds—as well as top honors in the 800-meter freestyle relay—in the 1936 games.

The Japanese swimming dominance disappeared completely after the 1936 games as the United States returned to prominence and another formidable swimming force emerged from Down Under.

POSTWAR GLORY

The 1936 games were to be the last Olympics for 12 years. In 1939, Europe became bitterly divided as the Allied forces took on Hitler's empire. World War II lasted six years and finally ended in victory for the Allies when Germany surrendered in 1945. Three years later the Olympics resumed, with nations once again gathering—this time in London—to compete against one another peacefully.

The hiatus served the American swimmers well. The U.S. men won all six gold medals at the 1948 games, and the five individual medals went to five different men. In the 100-meter freestyle, Walter Ris captured gold by defeating fellow countryman Alan Ford by half a second.

William Smith set an Olympic record in the 400-meter freestyle, winning the race in 4.41 minutes. The victory was a triumph for Smith, who had been stricken with typhus as a child and taken up swimming to rebuild his body. Smith swam to gold by defeating fellow U.S. swimmer James McLane by more than two hundredths of a second. McLane, however, would have his day, winning top honors in the 1500-meter freestyle. Seventeen years old at the time, McLane earned his victory through physical strength and sound strategy. He noticed his rival, John Marshall of Australia, tended to swim close to his left lane line. McLane purposely swam close to his own lane line on Marshall's right and kept one length ahead of him. This strategy distracted Marshall because McLane's powerful kick constantly splashed water in his face. McLane's plan propelled him to victory as he finished almost two tenths of a second ahead of Marshall.

In the 100-meter backstroke, Allen Stack swam almost a second and a half slower than his own world record time of 1:04.0, but still fast enough to beat countryman and second-place finisher Albert Vendewcghe by a tenth of a second. Joseph Verdeur took top honors in the 200-meter breaststroke by using the newly formed butterfly stroke, as did fellow Americans Keith Carter and Robert Sohl, the second- and third-place finishers. And Ris,

McLane, and Wallace Wolf romped to gold in the 800-meter freestyle relay, setting a world record of 8:46 in the process.

EMERGENCE OF THE DOWN UNDER SWIMMERS

The Americans once again fielded a strong team at the 1952 games in Helsinki, Finland. U.S. swimmers took home four gold medals. But few people watching the games would have guessed that the next national powerhouse in the sport would be from another hemisphere.

Swimming was always a sport of national prominence in Australia, and in some ways, its reemergence as a top swimming power was fitting. The Australians won only one gold medal in swimming during the Helsinki games, delivered by John Davies, who set an Olympic record time of 2:34:4 in the 200-meter breaststroke. Four years later, however, was quite another story. The swimmers from Down Under, competing in front of an enthusiastic and fiercely loyal home crowd in Melbourne, captured five out of seven swimming gold medals. The year 1956 marked the premiere of the 200-meter butterfly event and was won by American William Yorzyk. The addition of this race raised the total number of swimming events to seven. Australia's Jon Hendricks, winner of the 100-meter freestyle race, was the heavy favorite to take the gold. He rose to the occasion, setting an Olympic record and capturing his 56th win at that distance in 57 starts over a three-year period.

The second-place finisher in the 100-meter freestyle was Hendricks' countryman John Devitt, who would go on to set a world record in the event a year later. But Devitt may best be remembered as the winner of this event at the 1960 Olympics in Rome in one of the most controversial races in Olympic history. Devitt and Lance Larson of the United States had finished in what appeared to be a dead heat. When the six judges were consulted, three ruled that Larson had won and three gave the race to Devitt. According to the electronic timer, Larson had beaten Devitt by less than a tenth of a second, but the chief judge overruled the timing device, declared Devitt the victor. Larson protested the decision but it was not overturned.

The longer freestyle races at the Melbourne games belonged to a 17-year-old Australian named Murray Rose. His speed, as well as his choice of cuisine, earned him the nickname "Seaweed Streak," and he proved himself worthy of the moniker by slicing through the water in Olympic record time to capture gold in the 400-meter freestyle race. He defended his championship successfully in Rome four years later, breaking his own Olympic mark by more than 10 seconds in the process.

Rose also won the 1500-meter freestyle event in Melbourne, as well as a third gold medal in the 800-meter freestyle relay. Although he briefly held the world record in the 1500-meter freestyle, Rose fell short in his effort to win the event in Rome, finishing second to his teammate John Konrads.

DON SCHOLLANDER

Although swimming had its share of exhilarating races and charismatic champions during the 1930s, 1940s, and 1950s, the sport

lacked a dominating presence, a swimming superstar such as Weismuller or Kahanamoku. But all that changed with the emergence of a single swimmer who made Olympic history. The year was 1964 and the place was Tokyo, Japan. The swimmer was Donald Schollander, the first swimmer to win four gold medals at one Olympic Games.

Born in 1946 in Charlotte, North Carolina, Schollander was raised in Lake Oswego, Oregon, and trained in Santa Clara, California, under legendary swim coach George Haines. When Schollander went to Tokyo at the age of 18 to swim for America in 1964, he was already a world-record holder. One year earlier, Schollander had swum the fastest-ever 200-meter freestyle, recording a time of 1:54:3. Although the 200-meter freestyle was not an Olympic event in 1964, it was raced at the Tokyo games. The heavy favorite in this event, he rose to the occasion and cruised to an easy gold medal, breaking his own world record by half a second in the process.

The setup was slightly different in the 100-meter freestyle. Schollander was not as strong a sprinter as he was a middle-distance swimmer and for the final of this sprinting event, he found himself pitted against the current world record holder, Alain Gottvalles of France. Schollander found himself well ahead of Gottvalles (who was to finish fifth) at the halfway mark of the race, but trailing Great Britain's Robert McGregor. Schollander passed McGregor in the last five meters of the race and won by a tenth of a second, and his winning effort of 53.4 seconds was good enough for an Olympic record.

Schollander also won two team gold medals at the 1964 games. Swimming the anchor leg of the 800-meter relay, Schollander touched the wall to finish in 7:54:1. It was the first 800-meter relay to be swum in less than eight minutes. In fact, Schollander and his teammates' Olympic effort broke their own world record by more than eight seconds. He also anchored the American team in the 400-meter relay. This was the first Olympics in which the 400-meter relay was raced, and Schollander and crew christened the event by swimming it in a world record time of 3:32:2.

Schollander flew home from Tokyo with three world records, one Olympic record, and four gold medals in his pocket. He went on to win two more medals at the 1968 games in Mexico City, but it was his four-medal performance in Tokyo that set a new standard of excellence for swimmers. It was this mark that one swimmer in particular made it his own personal goal to surpass. That swimmer was Mark Spitz.

Don Schollander of Oswego Lake, Oregon, with the four gold medals he won at the 1964 Tokyo Olympics.

ALL ABOUT MARK

Mark Spitz was not the world's most popular man in 1968. That was the year the 18-year-old swimmer announced to his Olympic teammates and America that he would better Don Schollander's record haul of four gold medals in one Olympics and bring home six from Mexico City.

But Spitz was able to win only two golds, and both of them in team races. He managed a silver in the 100-meter butterfly, but accepted it bitterly. He won a bronze in the 100-meter freestyle, but in the 200-meter butterfly Spitz finished a dismal last in the finals. Moreover, his time of 2:13:5 was a full eight seconds slower than the world record mark of 2:05:7 which Spitz himself had set.

Clearly, Spitz had lost concentration and confidence by this last race. It wasn't the first time this had happened to an Olympian, but for Spitz, it was more difficult to take because of his brash predictions. Triumph would come to Spitz, but it would have to wait four more years.

Teammates Jerry Heidenreich (left) and Tom Bruce carry Mark Spitz on their shoulders after winning the gold medal in the 4 x 100-meter medley swimming event at the 1972 Olympics.

THE ROAD TO GLORY

It takes a lot of confidence for anyone to predict success in an Olympic event. The finest swimmers from around the world gather to compete in front of millions of spectators who watch the event live on television. What gave Mark Spitz the assurance to make such a claim?

He was talented. In fact, he was so gifted a swimmer that his coach at Indiana University called him "the greatest talent that ever pulled on a swimsuit." In addition, he had the training and background that was necessary for any champion swimmer.

Mark Spitz was born on February 10, 1950, in Modesto, California. His father, Arnold, stressed early and often to his son that "swimming isn't everything—winning is." And the elder Spitz was willing to back his philosophy with action. The family moved more than once during Mark's childhood so that the young swimmer could train under the guidance of the finest coaches in the sport.

Spitz had begun swimming competitively by age eight. He attended high school in several different parts of northern California, and starred on the swim team at each school. Mark Spitz used a mixture of sheer talent and surprise. He often swam his competitive meets much faster than he did his practices, which confused teammates and opponents alike. In addition, he had what was recognized as a flawless stroke efficiency. In other words, hands and legs worked together to propel him forward with top efficiency. Although he could swim any stroke, his two specialties were the butterfly and the freestyle. Nine years after his first competitive race, he swam to victories in the 1967 Pan American games, shattering two world records in his wake.

Little wonder, then, that Spitz thought he could take top honors at Mexico City. For anyone else, a total of four medals in one Olympics would never be considered a failure. But for Spitz, with the words of his father ringing in his ears, it clearly was. The disappointment of 1968 did not discourage him, however, but motivated him toward higher goals. The sign of a true champion, Mark Spitz lowered his head and went to work, his sights set on Munich in 1972.

BETWEEN THE GAMES

At age 18, Mark Spitz enrolled in Indiana University as a predental student.

The choice was a wise one for Spitz. His studies prepared him for what he thought would be his future career, and the swimming program at Indiana was top flight. His coach, James "Doc" Councilman, helped train Mark for what he knew would be the most important two weeks of his life. Councilman later said that what set Spitz apart from other swimmers was more than sheer talent. "[Few give Mark] credit for persistence," Councilman said of his protégé. "Once he had a target, he could go for it with more focus than I've ever seen."

Clearly, Spitz's focus was on victory. He strove to win at Indiana and to do it with skills, not boasts. There would be no brash predictions or promises of glory, and his newfound humility endeared him to his teammates. In addition, he led Indiana to three consecutive NCAA titles and in doing so learned about teamwork and leadership. These were qualities that would serve him well as he trained for his ultimate goal of Olympic victory.

ON TO MUNICH

Spitz was a mature 22-year old at the time of the Olympic trials. His performance not

Mark Spitz displays his familiar victory sign after winning one of seven gold medals at the 1972 Munich Olympics.

only earned him a spot on the team headed to Munich, but also caught the attention of the press who remembered his predictions from the 1968 games. Although Mark did not speak much to journalists about what he planned to do in Munich, speculation grew that he could come away with as many as seven gold medals.

The first race in that lineup was in many ways the most loaded. The 200-meter butterfly was the race that had humiliated Spitz the most (he was the last-place finisher in that race in the Mexico City Olympics). But soon after that fiasco, Spitz had broken his own world record in the event, swimming the four lengths in 2:01:53. He was the odds-on favorite for gold.

Mark was understandably nervous on the starting blocks, waiting for the signal to start. But once the gun went off, there was no doubt who would emerge victorious. Spitz led the race from beginning to end, beating the second-place finisher by almost two seconds and breaking his own world record in the process. His victorious time for the race was an unprecedented 2:00:7.

With one victory under his belt, Spitz relaxed and felt more confident. He sailed through his second race, the 400-meter freestyle relay, with a new world record, and won his third, the 200-meter freestyle. In this race, he was in second place with 50 meters to go, but overtook teammate Steven Genter and touched poolside in world record time of 1:52:78. Three golds and three world records in two days. Mark Spitz was off to an impressive start.

MAKING HISTORY

Spitz won his fourth gold in the 100-meter butterfly, in which he set a new mark in the race (and broke his old one) with a time of 54:27. At this point, world records were falling as rapidly as gold medals were piling up. Later that day he won his fifth, swimming the anchor leg of the 800-meter freestyle relay, and set a new world record. Then, with five golds behind him and only two more races to go, Mark Spitz got cold feet.

His teammate Jerry Heidenreich was swimming in top form, and Spitz found himself wondering if it was worth the effort to try to compete against him. Perhaps he was experi-

Mark Spitz surges ahead to win his heat in the men's 200-meter butterfly event at the 1972 Munich Olympics. Spitz set a new world record of 2:00.7 in the final. He won an unprecedented seven gold medals along with setting as many new world records.

encing flashbacks of Mexico City, or maybe he did not want to press his luck.

Spitz did decide to swim the 100-meter freestyle, but swam his qualifying heats conservatively, finishing behind Heidenreich as well as Michael Wenden, who had defeated him for the gold in the same event in Mexico City. In the end, Spitz turned on the power and the speed. He stunned Heidenreich by forgoing his usual strategy of starting slowly and finishing fast; instead, he steamed into the water and churned through the first length of the race well ahead of the pack. Spitz was clearly in the lead going into the final turn of the race. But suddenly, he lost his rhythm in the final 15 meters. With Heidenreich catching up and the rest of the field not far behind, Spitz recovered quickly and beat Heidenreich to the wall by almost four tenths of a second for his sixth gold medal of the games and his sixth world record. Spitz's time in the race was 51.22, two and one-half tenths of a second faster than his old mark of 51.47.

TRIUMPH AND TRAGEDY

The next day, Spitz sailed to his seventh and final gold, setting a new world record of 3:48:16 in the 400-meter medley relay. After his victory, he felt like celebrating, and went out for dinner with friends. He returned to his room at two o'clock in the morning.

Several hours later, news of a stunning tragedy spread through Olympic village. In the early hours of September 5th, 1972, armed Arab terrorists snuck into the complex housing Israeli athletes and began shooting. An athlete and a coach were killed immediately and nine athletes taken hostage. The terrorists demanded release of 200 Arabs held in Israeli and German prisons and safe passage to an Arab country.

When the terrorists and their hostages arrived at the airbase to board an outward-bound plane, trained German marksmen opened fire in an effort to rescue the hostages and capture the terrorists. In the ensuing shootout, one policeman and three terrorists were killed. The remaining terrorists, pinned down, tossed a hand grenade into the helicopter that held the hostages. All nine athletes were killed. All told, eleven Israelis, one policemen, and five terrorists had died in the most harrowing event in all Olympic history.

Although this event marked the end of the celebrations, Mark Spitz's achievements in Munich remain one of the highlights of Olympic history, a true victory of persistence and perseverance that put him above all other swimmers.

MARK SPITZ TODAY

After the 1972 games, Spitz returned to the United States a celebrity. His dark good looks earned him many endorsement contracts, and he used the money he earned to open a real estate development business.

Today, his world records have all been broken, and the world of swimming has moved on. Nevertheless, Mark Spitz will always be remembered for his triumphs in Munich. His performance there earned him a legitimate claim of being perhaps the best swimmer in American—and maybe even world—history.

THE AMERICANS DOMINATE

4

In 1979, the Soviet Union invaded the country of Afghanistan in an attempt to add it to its legion of communist nations. The democratic nations, headed by the United States, marked their opposition to this move by refusing to attend the 1980 Olympics in Moscow. Four years later, the Soviet Union and its communist allies (with the exception of Romania) returned the favor by boycotting the 1984 games in Los Angeles. It was not until the 1988 games in Seoul, Korea, that the communist and capitalist countries once again competed against each other. By that time, the cold war had ended, and so, too, had the Olympic boycotts, except for Cuba, which has boycotted every Olympics held on the soil of a democratic nation since the 1984 Los Angeles games.

JOHN NABER

John Naber's achievements at the Montreal games were reminiscent of Mark Spitz's at Munich. He was an expert at two strokes in the same domineering way that Spitz was, and like Mark he was tall and good-looking, complete with dark hair and mustache. Naber's specialties were the freestyle and the backstroke, and he would compete in both events in his first and, as it turned out, his only Olympics.

If Spitz was outspoken about his desire to win six golds in Munich, Naber was much more

John Naber, U.S. swimmer, sets a new world record during the 100-meter backstroke final at the 1976 Olympics in Montreal, taking the gold medal.

reticent about his goal for Montreal. What Naber really wanted to accomplish in 1976 was to beat an East German swimmer by the name of Roland Matthes. The champion of the 100- and 200-meter backstroke events at the 1968 and 1972 games, Matthes was Naber's idol, as well as his archrival. He was the man Naber had never beaten. In Montreal, the stage was set for a showdown in the backstroke event.

Naber's quest for gold had begun several years earlier. As a high school swimmer in Woodside, California, the 16-year-old Naber was training for a spot on the Olympic team for 1972. Unfortunately, his dream was cut short when he broke his collarbone in a diving board accident. Naber was out of his cast by the time of the trials, but the injury had cost him valuable training time. Unfortunately, he missed making the Olympic team by six tenths of a second.

Two years later, Naber was back in form and swimming well going into the 1974 USA-East German Dual Meet. He was looking forward to racing against Matthes, who had not been beaten in seven years. The year before, in Belgrade, Naber finished third to him. The Dual Meet was John Naber's chance for revenge. And the taste was sweet.

He beat the East German soundly in both the 100- and 200-meter backstroke events, effectively putting an end to Matthes' domination. But Naber was not satisfied. Matthes had swum below par at the meet because he was suffering from the aftereffects of root canal surgery and could not find his rhythm. Moreover, although Naber had beaten Matthes

in their head-to-head competition, he had not broken any of the East German's records.

John Naber was out to beat those records. As he trained for the Olympics, he thought endlessly about Matthes' times. Could he beat them? In addition to the backstroke, Naber decided to compete in the 200-meter freestyle event, the final of which was scheduled, as luck would have it, 45 minutes after the final of the 100-meter backstroke event. Naber qualified easily for the backstroke event, and made it by the skin of his nose to the finals of the 200-meter freestyle (his time was eighth best among all qualifiers, good enough for the final spot).

Naber sailed to victory in the finals of the 100-meter backstroke race. He not only beat Matthes, but also shattered the East German's world record, swimming the final in 55.49. This world record would stand for an astonishing seven years before being broken in 1983 by American Rick Carey. After beating Matthes, Naber took a quick rubdown, slept

John Naber of the U.S. swimming team in his leg of the men's 4 x 100-meter medley relay at the 1976 Olympics, in which his team won the gold medal.

for 10 minutes, and got on the starting blocks for the final of the 200-meter freestyle. Naber's time of 1:50:50 was better than the existing world record, but only good enough to win him a silver. American Bruce Furniss nabbed the gold by swimming the race in world-record time of 1:50:29. Even so, Naber considered this race among his proudest achievements.

He went on to win the 200-meter backstroke as well. Matthes, who won the silver in the 100-meter event, did not figure in this race because he had suffered an attack of appendicitis prior to the event. But Naber went after Matthes all the same, intending to shatter the East German's world record time of 2:02:8. And shatter it he did. In his gold medal performance, Naber broke the world record, and became the first swimmer to complete the race in less than two minutes. Naber's Montreal mark of 1:59:19 remained unbroken until 1983. And no one would swim the 200-meter backstroke under two minutes at an Olympic contest again until 1988, when Igor Polyanski of the Soviet Union finished in 1:59:37.

Naber also won gold in the 400-meter freestyle relay and in the backstroke leg of the 400-meter medley relay. All told, Naber took home four golds and a silver in one Olympics.

ROWDY GAINES

If Rowdy Gaines could change anything about his life, he would no doubt say that he wishes he could have swum in the 1980 games in Moscow. Twenty-one at the time, Gaines was at the top of his sport. He was the holder of the 200-meter freestyle record in 1980 and at the brink of setting a record in the 100-meter freestyle.

When the decision was announced that the United States would not compete in Moscow, Gaines did not give up his sport, but determined instead to remain in his prime for four more years until he could compete for gold in the Los Angeles games in 1984. To stay on top of his game, Gaines swam in swim event after swim event in 1981, 1982, and 1983. He broke his own world record in the 200-meter freestyle in 1982, and broke the record for the 100-meter freestyle three times, holding it until 1985.

Most male swimmers, however, are in their prime between the ages of 21 and 23. By the time Gaines had the opportunity to swim in the Olympics again, he was 25 years old. Only one of the 67 competitors at the Los Angeles games was older than Gaines, but none was more determined.

Gaines concentrated his talents on the 100-meter freestyle event. He made the Olympic squad by finishing second to Mike Heath at the trials, but entered the Olympics feeling unsure about his chances at the gold. Gaines had actually gone so far as to write a concession speech that he would make to the press after losing the event. Fortunately for Gaines, this move proved to be premature. Gaines' coach, Richard Quick, gave some brilliant advice to his swimmer before the start of the final. Quick had noticed that the official starter for the 100-meter event was always quick to pull the trigger. Standing on the starting block, Gaines remembered this observa-

Rowdy Gaines celebrates his win after the U.S. team took the gold medal in the 4 x 100-meter freestyle event at the 1984 Los Angeles Olympics.

tion, and prepared himself for a fast start. As soon as the starting gun sounded (almost immediately after the "swimmers take your mark" announcement) Gaines was off the blocks and swimming. His start propelled him to a fast first lap and he stayed in the lead for the entire race, winning the gold in Olympic record time of 49:80.

Rowdy Gaines left Los Angeles with two more golds, one in the 400-meter freestyle relay and the other in the 400-meter medley relay. He would not medal in the 200-meter freestyle race, but his three gold-medal performances in 1984 went a long way toward healing the disappointment he felt for not competing in the 1980 games.

MATT BIONDI

A long-time resident of California, Matt Biondi idolized 1972 Olympic champion Mark Spitz. Little did he know that he, himself, would one day bring home seven medals from one Olympics in the single greatest performance by a male swimmer since Mark Spitz.

Although Biondi admired swimmers, he did not himself become one until the relatively late age of 15. A sophomore in high school in Moraga, California, Biondi played basketball and water polo in addition to participating in swimming races. He trained equally hard in all three sports, but it was swimming that catapulted him to sudden recognition. Out of the blue in 1984—three years after he started swimming competitively—Matt Biondi made the Olympic swimming team and went to Los Angeles to compete.

In Los Angeles, Biondi got his first taste of Olympic gold. Swimming the third leg in the 400-meter freestyle relay team, he helped set a new world record in the event. After the games ended, he entered the University of California, where he continued to swim competitively and to play water polo.

Four years later, Matt Biondi qualified for his second Olympic team, and flew with his fellow Americans to compete for gold in Seoul, Korea. This time, however, his success was no surprise. Famous for his collegiate achievements, he came to Seoul a heavy favorite to win medals in seven events.

And like Mark Spitz before him, Matt Biondi lived up to his advance billing. In the 50-meter freestyle—an event that had not been swum in the Olympics since the 1904 St. Louis games—he competed against fellow countryman and world record holder Tom Jager, an undergraduate at UCLA. Biondi and Jager had faced one another 14 times in this event, and Jager emerged triumphant 10 of those times. Moreover, Biondi had not beaten

Matt Biondi wins his heat of the 100-meter butterfly competition at the 1988 Olympics.

Jager in this event in two years. He broke through in stellar fashion, however, defeating Jager by 18 tenths of a second to take gold and setting a world record of 22.14 in the process.

In the 100-meter freestyle, Biondi was the heavy favorite, having already recorded the ten fastest times in this event in history. Even so, he could easily have been shaken at the pressure going into this event. He could also have been feeling vulnerable; he had just finished second in the 100-meter butterfly final earlier in the day, losing the gold by one-hundredth of a second. Biondi made up for this disappointment by swimming a stellar 48.63 in the 100-meter freestyle, slightly over his world record time of 48.42 and good enough for a new Olympic record and a gold medal.

Matt Biondi added three more gold medals to his collection by winning the 800-meter freestyle relay, the 400-meter freestyle relay, and the 400-meter medley relay. Biondi's bronze came in the 200-meter freestyle relay, where he finished more than half a second behind the first place finisher, an Australian named Duncan Armstrong, who set a world record in the process.

Matt Biondi returned to the Olympics in 1992 and won a team gold in the 400-meter freestyle relay. By doing so, he became only the sixth American male swimmer in history to compete in three Olympic Games.

MICHAEL GROSS

In an era of heavy American domination in the sport of swimming, a name from another country stands out as a champion in his own

West Germany's record swimmer Michael Gross in action during the 100-meter butterfly heats at the 1984 Los Angeles Olympics.

right. Michael Gross has graced the record books as holder of the fastest times in two events, the only swimmer to hold that distinction other than Mark Spitz.

At 6 feet 7 inches, Gross was an awesome and intimidating sight at the Los Angeles Olympics in 1984. In the 200-meter freestyle, Gross mowed down his competition when he beat second-place finisher Michael Heath of the United States by a full second and a half to secure his first gold. In addition, he shattered his own world mark in the event, swimming the race in a stunning time of 1:47:44.

The race made history for Gross. In addition to setting a new world record, he distinguished himself by becoming the first West German to win an Olympic swimming event. Although Germany had historically been a powerhouse in the sport of swimming, much of the glory for that nation came before the country was split into West and East in 1961. Since that time, all Olympic swimming champions from Germany were officially from communist East Germany. Gross broke that precedent, albeit in an Olympic Games boycotted by all communist nations. Even so, his world record in the 200-meter freestyle proved beyond a shadow of a doubt that Gross was the fastest swimmer in that event during his time.

In addition to his record-breaking performance in the 200-meter freestyle event, Gross added another gold—and another world record—in the 100-meter butterfly. This race was swum so quickly that the top six racers all set national records. But top honors went to Gross, who sliced through the water in 53:08. His new record bested the old one by three tenths of a second. The holder of that former world record, who finished second to Gross in the race in Los Angeles, would have his day in the sun eight years later. His name is Pablo Morales.

PABLO MORALES

After finishing second to Michael Gross in Los Angeles, Pablo Morales contemplated the current situation. He had been the world record holder of the 100-meter butterfly, and had just swum that Olympic race faster than ever before in his life. Even so, his performance was good enough only for second place as Gross shattered all previous marks to take the gold. One thought gave him comfort, however: there would be another Olympic race in four years. In 1988 he would have his revenge.

Unfortunately, the Seoul games proved to be unlucky for Morales. He was unable to accompany the team to Korea because he finished third in the qualifying heat for the race at the U.S. Olympic trials. Because only the top two finishers of a race at the trials can represent their team at the Olympics, Pablo had to watch the games on television from his home in the United States.

After failing to make the Olympic team, Morales retired from swimming to attend law school at Cornell University but soon missed the rigor and excitement of competing. He returned to the pool in the summer of 1991 and trained long hours in hopes of making the Barcelona Olympics. His hard work paid off. He made the squad and flew to Barcelona with his teammates, intent on making up for his disappointing finish in the 1984 games.

Morales stood nervously at the starting block for the 100-meter butterfly. This was the moment for which he had prepared over the past eight years.

When the starting gun went off, Morales was slow to leave the starting platform, but he took the lead by the end of the first length and went on to win the race. While standing on the victory stand, Morales later told reporters that he was thinking about his mother who had died of cancer in the summer of 1991: "My mother would want to be here to experience this, and I know that she was with me in spirit. This was my time at last."

Morales' gold medal in the 100-meter butterfly may have been his biggest triumph, but it was not his only one. He captured a second gold in the butterfly leg of the 400-meter medley. Two gold medals in one Olympic competition. Not bad for a 27-year-old law student!

Pablo Morales raises his arm in jubilation after winning the gold medal in the 100-meter butterfly event at the 1992 Olympic games.

THE GREATEST OF EASE

5

I f you ever jumped off a diving board, you probably have an appreciation for this most graceful of sports in which athletes defy gravity and overcome fear. Diving is a sport that looks frightening, and in reality it is. But when done right, it is a beautiful event to watch and is, perhaps, the most thrilling of all Olympic events.

TYPES OF DIVES

An appreciation of diving begins with a definition of its terms and an explanation of its rules and regulations.

There are two types of diving events. The first is the springboard event which takes place on a "springy" diving board three meters (9 feet, 10 inches) above the water. The second is platform diving. It is held on a high, motionless platform ten meters (32 feet, 9½ inches) above the water.

Each type of dive is performed in one of three positions. First is the straight position, in which the body remains straight up and down. Second is the tuck position, in which the body is bent at the knees and hips and the knees are held together against the chest. Third is the pike position, in which the body is bent at the waist and the legs are straight. Although the diver's body may assume any of these positions while in the air, he or she always straightens out before entering the water head first with legs straight, feet together, and toes pointed.

Klaus Dibiasi of Italy leaves the 10-meter platform in a tuck position and enters the water straight as an arrow, winning the gold medal at the 1968 Olympics. Dibiasi also won the gold in the 1972 and 1976 Olympics.

There are six different dives in competitive diving. A forward dive means that the diver faces the front of the board and rotates toward the water. Forward dives range in difficulty from the simple front dive most novices learn to do first, to a four-and-one-half somersault expert dive, performed only by top athletes. A back dive means that at the beginning of the dive, the diver stands at the end of the board with his or her back to the water, then jumps backward, rotating away from the board. A reverse dive is a dive that begins with the diver facing the front of the board, then jumping away from the board but rotating backward, toward the board. An inward dive occurs when the diver stands in the same position as a back dive, but instead of rotating away from the board, the diver's body arches toward the board. A twisting dive is simply a dive in which the competitor twists his or her body in the same direction. Finally, there is the armstand position, in which the diver begins the dive in a handstand position at the edge of the dive. This type of dive is performed only in platform competition, and is much less common now than it once was. Any type of dive can include a twisting motion: in fact, the great majority of Olympic dives do include twists.

WHAT THE JUDGES LOOK FOR

Similar to ice skating and gymnastics, diving is a sport scored by judges. The winners of sports such as swimming or running are determined simply by who finishes a given distance in the fastest time. Champions of these types of sports are obvious: they are the athletes who break the ribbon first or touch the side of the pool before the others. Diving, however, is less clear-cut. Each dive is witnessed by a panel of seven officials who score the dive according to certain factors. At the end of the competition, the diver with the highest score is declared the winner.

There are a number of elements that judges look for to determine the score for a certain dive. First, there is the approach to the dive, the three or four steps taken by the diver to reach the end of the board. Next is the takeoff, the actual jump from the board. The takeoff should be strong, confident, and always with feet together and toes pointed. Approaches are seen only in forward (or front) and reverse dives, but takeoffs are a part of every dive.

Judges also look at the height an athlete reaches after the takeoff. In general, the higher a diver is able to jump off the board the better his or her score will be. In addition to a better score, greater height gives a diver more time and space to perform the twists and turns that make up the dive.

Then there is the execution of the dive. Executing a dive successfully means performing it with proper technique and skill. Excellent form, along with a certain amount of beauty and grace from the beginning of the dive to its ending, are all important elements in the final scoring. The last element judges look for is known as the entry. Entry occurs at the end of a dive when the athlete enters the water. A diver should enter the water in as close to a straight up and down, or vertical, position as is possible. Toes should always be pointed. If a diver enters the water head first, the arms should be stretched above the head

Dr. Sammy Lee, in perfect form, dives from the tower at the 1948 Olympic platform diving competition.

with hands together. A diver entering the water feet first should have legs and feet straight together, with arms held rigid and close to the body, and toes pointed.

Judges look at the amount of "splash" that results from the diver entering the water. The more straight up-and-down he or she is, the less splash there will be. The best entries—the ones with little splash—are referred to as "rips" because of the tearing sound a diver makes when entering the water.

A BRIEF HISTORY

Diving began in 17th century Sweden and Germany as a form of training for gymnastics. These athletes found it useful to practice their flips, somersaults, and twists over water, which provided a softer landing than a hard floor. This form of practice was particularly popular during the summer months, when gymnasts could train at the beach. In the late 19th century, diving officially broke away from gymnastics to form its own sport, although it was often included in gymnastics competitions as recently as the 1920s.

The first diving competitions took place in Great Britain in 1893, and two years later, a yearly competitive event was formed by the Royal Life Saving Society of Great Britain. This annual competition continued until 1961. By then diving had become a popular Olympic event. The first Olympic diving competition was held at the 1904 games in St. Louis when Dr. George Sheldon of the United States took home the gold in the first platform competition. Four years later in London, Albert Zurner of Germany became the first springboard

Olympic diving champion. The women's platform event became an Olympic event in 1912 and the women's springboard in 1920.

Diving is a sport that has historically been dominated by Americans. From 1920 through 1992, Americans won springboard gold in every Olympic Games except 1972 and 1980. Perhaps the greatest diver of all time was American Greg Louganis. But other champions of the sport who came before him also made their mark.

SAMMY LEE

Sammy Lee was a first-class diver who won Olympic gold medals in the springboard diving events of 1948 and 1952.

Lee was 28 years of age when he won the first of those golds in the 1948 games in London. A doctor with the American army at the time, Lee was a Korean-American competing in his first Olympic competition. His last dive was his most difficult one: a forward three and one-half somersault in the tuck position. As frightening as that dive sounds to a beginner, it was even more so for Sammy Lee. At an earlier competition, he had become confused during mid-dive, mixing up sky and water. He bailed out of the dive midway through, and was charged with a failed dive. Standing on the platform in London, he vowed not to make the same mistake. He jumped in the air and completed his dive. After his entry, he swam to the edge of the pool, unsure of how he had done. "I dove, hit the water, felt numb and tingling, and decided, I did a belly flop." But Lee had performed a near perfect dive. It helped him make history as he became the first Asian-American to win Olympic gold.

Dr. Sammy Lee, U.S. Army medical lieutenant, hits the water in gold medal form during the 1948 Olympic high diving finals.

Four years later, Lee made history again when he won the platform event by a full nine points on his 32nd birthday.

KLAUS DIBIASI

Known as *"Angelo Biondo,"* or the "blonde angel," Italian-born Klaus Dibiasi dominated platform diving over three consecutive Olympics, earning golds in the Mexico City, Munich, and Montreal games in 1968, 1972, and 1976. Diving for Dibiasi was a family legacy as well as a personal passion. Coached by his father, Carlo, the 10th-place diver at the 1936 Berlin games, he grew up practicing 130 to 150 dives a day, six days a week.

The endless practices paid off as Dibiasi made it to his first Olympic games in Tokyo in 1964 and captured a silver medal in the platform diving event. Four years later in Mexico City, Dibiasi was even more impressive, capturing a gold in the platform event and a silver in the springboard competition. He impressed the diving world with his "no splash" water entrances, also known as rip entries. Dibiasi's first-place finish in 1968 marked the first gold medal ever won by an Italian in swimming or diving competitions.

His stunning form and technique was good enough to capture gold again four years later in Munich, but by 1976, most people thought Dibiasi was past his prime and ready to pass the mantle. Dibiasi proved his critics wrong, however, and landed an unprecedented (and still unmatched) third consecutive gold medal in the platform competition. Finishing second to Dibiasi—by more than 24 points—was a young man from California. That diver would

Klaus Dibiasi goes after a gold medal in the 10-meter platform diving finals at the 1968 Olympics.

go on to completely dominate diving in a remarkable fashion, in a way that will probably never be duplicated. The young man's name was Greg Louganis.

THE GREATEST
OF THEM ALL

6

Who would have thought that anyone—even champion Greg Louganis—would have the confidence to attempt the world's most difficult dive one year after witnessing another diver become fatally injured while trying the same thing? But he did. The year was 1984 and the place was Los Angeles. Louganis stood on the 10-meter platform, preparing to jump forward, pull his legs to his chest in a tuck position, and flip backward three and one-half times. The dive, the three-and-one-half reverse somersault, was known to insiders as "the dive of death." In 1983, Louganis had seen the unthinkable happen. A Soviet diver attempting the dive hit his head on the platform and fell into the water. One week later the diver had died.

As Louganis stood on the platform, he put the tragedy out of his mind. He had other things to think about. This was to be his 10th and final dive. He needed to perform it well enough to clinch the gold medal and push his final score past the 700 mark, a plateau no diver had ever been able to surpass.

Louganis leaped into the air, and with knees against his chest, flipped precisely three and one half times and entered the water head first with barely a ripple in his wake. The crowd roared. The judges took little time in posting their reactions. One perfect 10, the rest all 9s and 9.5s. Louganis had done it. His final score was more

Greg Louganis competes for a gold medal in the finals of the men's springboard at the 1984 Olympics.

than 10 points above the 700 mark. It was his most triumphant moment to date, but it was not his only one. Several days earlier, Greg had demolished the competition in the springboard event to claim his first gold medal of the 1984 games. He had won both diving events in a fashion never witnessed before or since in Olympic competition and he had made diving history.

CHILDHOOD PAIN

Greg Louganis' story began in 1960, when he was born to unmarried parents who gave him up for adoption to commercial fisherman Peter Louganis and his wife, Frances. Greg grew up taking gymnastics and dancing classes with his older sister. At the age of six, he could tap dance as well as many professionals. But he had his share of troubles. He had a great deal of difficulty learning to read and this hardship cost him dearly because he could not keep up with his schoolmates' achievements, which took its toll on his self-confidence. What no one knew at the time was that Louganis suffered from dyslexia, a common learning disability that makes reading difficult. During this time, Louganis suffered from feelings of self-doubt and was teased relentlessly by classmates, who made fun of his dark skin and his learning difficulties. He soon found solace in drugs and alcohol and began to smoke cigarettes when he was nine and marijuana when he was twelve.

Fortunately for Louganis, he had his athletic skills to combat some of his pain. Eventually, he overcame his alcoholism, and devoted himself to the world of diving. It was the most important decision of Louganis' life.

TEENAGE PHENOMENON

Louganis began diving lessons as a child, and by the age of 11 he was good enough to compete in the junior national championships. He not only won the title, but also scored a perfect 10 in one of dives, a feat almost unheard of in junior diving competition.

His performance at the junior nationals won the attention of several college coaches and turned the head of former Olympic champion Sammy Lee, who took special note of the young Louganis' talent. He kept in touch with the youngster during his troubled times, and when Greg turned the corner at age 15, Lee agreed to become his coach.

In no time at all, Lee turned Louganis into an Olympic contender. In 1976, at the age of 16, Louganis made the Olympic diving team and went to Montreal to compete. From relative obscurity, Louganis stunned the diving world by finishing sixth in the springboard event. Even more impressive, he battled reigning Olympic champion Klaus Dibiasi in the platform event. Dibiasi emerged triumphant, but on the victory stand he hugged the young 16-year-old runner up. "Now I can sit back and watch you win in Moscow," the Italian champion said graciously, referring to the site of the 1980 Olympic Games.

Sadly for Louganis, there was no Moscow competition. America boycotted the 1980 games after the Soviet invasion of Afghanistan, and the 20-year-old Louganis would have to wait until 1984 for his quest for gold.

Greg Louganis in perfect form to win a gold medal in the springboard event in the 1984 Olympics in Los Angeles.

A CHAMPION COMES OF AGE

Disappointed but not discouraged by the American boycott, Louganis spent the time between Olympic games pursuing other interests. He enrolled at the University of California at Irvine, where he became an active member of the drama and dance programs. He was so immersed in his activities at Irvine that few of his classmates realized that he was a diving champion.

But in 1984, they would know. At the Los Angeles games he won by 94 points in the springboard event and 67 in the platform, scores almost unheard of in the world of diving where a 20-point victory was considered a rout.

At 24 years of age, Louganis was undeniably the king of diving. He briefly considered retiring while still at the top of his game, but changed his mind and decided to repeat both his victories at the 1988 games at Seoul. Louganis continued to compete in the years between the Los Angeles and Seoul games. He won several major titles, including the 1987 Pan American Games. He also continued to develop his dancing and acting talents and made his debut as a professional dancer in Indianapolis, where he won critical acclaim. But Louganis' major triumph was still ahead.

GOING FOR THE DOUBLE DOUBLE

When Greg Louganis won gold in both diving events in the 1984 games, he became the first competitor to do so since Peter Desjardin took top honors in both events in 1928. Master divers like Sammy Lee and Klaus Dibiasi had specialized in one event or the other. Moreover, no male diver had ever won both gold medals in two consecutive Olympic Games. The only person who ever achieved this "double double" was a woman diver named Pat McCormick who had taken top honors in both events in the 1952 and 1956 games.

Louganis, however, was a master of both the springboard and platform events, and was the favorite to win gold in both competitions at the Seoul games. The springboard competition was the first of the two diving events. Things were going smoothly for Louganis when all of a sudden, disaster struck. Louganis' ninth dive in the preliminary round was a reverse two-and-one-half somersault in the pike position. But during his takeoff, Louganis failed to jump far enough away from the diving board. His

Greg Louganis does a back 2-1/2 somersault from the pike position during springboard preliminaries at the 1984 Olympics.

head came down hard on the springboard and he fell awkwardly into the water.

Although he did not lose consciousness, his injury was serious enough to merit five stitches. Somehow, Louganis kept his confidence and concentration. Thirty-five minutes after the accident, Greg was back on the board about to perform his last dive of the preliminaries, another reverse somersault. This time, he cleared the board and soared into the water. His score for that dive of 87.12 was the highest of any diver in the preliminary round. He went on to victory in that event a day later, defeating Chinese diver Tan Liangde, who had beaten Louganis twice earlier in the year.

In the platform event Louganis was under intense scrutiny and pressure. Would his injury affect his concentration going off the high board? Would the thought of winning the double double overburden the veteran diver? Would the thought of this being perhaps his last competition (Louganis had hinted that he planned to retire after the Seoul games) prove to be unsettling? And what about his major competition for the event, 14-year-old Chinese diver Xiong Ni? Would the advantage of youth and obscurity be enough to defeat the reigning Olympic champion?

The competition began a bit slowly for Louganis. After four dives, he held a narrow lead over Xiong, but lost it the next round. With one dive to go, Louganis had to be close to perfect. He had to score at least 85.57 points out of a possible 90 to clinch the gold. The last dive on his list was the one that had taken the life of the Soviet diver years ago and the one Louganis had done perfectly in Los Angeles in 1984. Once again, Louganis stood on the platform, ready to perform the world's most difficult dive, the three-and-one-half reverse somersault.

Louganis contemplated the situation. He recalled the words of a reporter, who had told him that regardless of his heroic performance on the springboard, if he lost the gold on the platform, he would be considered a failure. But he consoled himself with thoughts that his mother would love him regardless of whether or not he won.

The dive was magnificent. The scores were sensational. Louganis had scored an 86.70, giving him a total of 638.61. It was good enough for gold and Xiong, with 637.47, was awarded the silver. Louganis had become the first man ever to win both diving golds in two consecutive games.

THE BATTLE OF HIS LIFE

For Louganis, the toughest battle lay ahead of him. After the 1988 games, he turned to acting, with some success, but seven years after Seoul his name was in the news again, this time for a completely different reason. Greg Louganis was infected with HIV, the virus that causes AIDS.

In 1995, he published his memoirs as *Breaking the Surface*, which tells of his battle with the disease. He began taking AZT, a medicine shown to slow the progress of the AIDS virus. Today, he continues his treatment and has become an outspoken advocate of the battle to find a treatment and cure for AIDS.

As of spring 1998 he remained in good condition. But regardless of the outcome, Greg Louganis will always be known for the sheer perfection and elegance of his work on the diving boards, and for his grace and dignity throughout all of his battles. We wish him all the best.

Greg Louganis,
a true champion.

CHRONOLOGY

4 B.C.	First water races held in Japan.
1875	Matthew Webb becomes the first person to swim across the English Channel.
1896	Hungarian swimmer Alfred Hajos wins Olympic gold at the 1896 games in Athens, Greece.
1904	First Olympic diving event is held at the St. Louis games.
1912	Hawaiian swimming champion Duke Kahanamoku wins a gold and a silver medal in the Stockholm games. First women's Olympic swimming races held.
1916	World War I forces cancellation of the summer Olympic Games.
1924	Johnny Weismuller wins three golds and a bronze for the Americans in the Paris games.
1932	Buster Crabbe wins Olympic gold at Los Angeles in the 400-meter freestyle event.
1936	Japanese male swimmers win four gold medals at the Berlin Olympics.
1940–44	The Olympic Games are cancelled by World War II.
1948	The Olympic Games resume in London three years after Germany's surrender.
1956	The butterfly stroke is raced for the first time in Olympic competition in Melbourne, where Australian male swimmers win five gold medals.
1964	At the Tokyo Olympics, Don Schollander becomes the first swimmer to win four gold medals in one Olympic Games.
1968	Klaus Dibiasi captures diving gold and silver in Mexico City.
1972	Mark Spitz wins a total of seven gold medals at the Munich games.
1980	The United States boycotts the Moscow games because of Russia's invasion of Afghanistan.
1984	Greg Louganis becomes the "king of diving" at the Los Angeles games by winning gold in both the platform and springboard events.
1984	Russia and its communist allies boycott the games in retaliation for the 1980 U.S. boycott.
1988	Matt Biondi wins seven medals and Greg Louganis repeats as platform and springboard diving champion at the Seoul Olympics.
1996	American male swimmers win six gold medals at the Atlanta Olympics.

FURTHER READING

Lewis, H. Carlson, and John J. Fogarty. *Tales of Gold*. Chicago: Contemporary Books, Inc., 1987.

Schaap, Dick. *Illustrated History of the Olympics*. New York: Knopf, 1963.

Wallechinsky, David. *SI Presents The Complete Book of the Olympics*. Boston: Little Brown, 1996.

Nelson, Rebecca, and Marie J. Macnee, ed. *The Olympic Handbook*. Detroit: Visible, Inc., 1996.

INDEX

Armstrong, Duncan, 40
Biondi, Matt, 38–40
Bruce, Tom, 24
Buetting, Kurt, 11
Carey, Rick, 35
Carter, Keith, 19
Cavill, Frederick, 10
Councilman, James "Doc", 27
Crabbe, Buster, 14–15, 17
Davies, John, 20
Devitt, John, 20–21
Dibiasi, Carlo, 50
Dibiasi, Klaus, 44, 50–52, 55, 57
Furniss, Bruce, 36
Gaines, Rowdy, 36–38
Genter, Steven, 28
Gottvalles, Alain, 22
Gross, Michael, 41–42
Hajos, Alfred, 7–8
Heath, Mike, 37, 41
Heidenreich, Jerry, 24, 29, 30
Hendricks, Jon, 20
Hitler, Adolf, 18
Irie, Toshio, 17
Jager, Tom, 39–40

Kahanamoku, Duke Paoa Kahinu
   Makoe Hulikohoa, 11-12, 13, 22
Kahanamoku, Sam, 13
Kawatsu, Kentaro, 17
Kitamura, Kusuo, 17
Kuyokawa, Mesaji, 17
Koike, Reizo, 17
Konrads, John, 21
Larson, Lance, 21
Lee, Sammy, 47, 49–50, 55, 57
Liangde, Tan, 58
Louganis, Frances, 54
Louganis, Greg, 49, 51–61
Louganis, Peter, 54
Marshall, John, 19
Matthes, Roland, 34–36
Mayazaki, Yasuji, 17
McCormick, Pat, 57
McGregor, Robert, 22
McLane, James, 19
Morales, Pablo, 42–43
Naber, John, 32–36
Ni, Xiong, 59
Owens, Jesse, 18
Polyanski, Igor, 36

Quick, Richard, 37
Ris, Walter, 19
Rose, Murray, 21
Schollander, Don, 21–23, 25
Sheldon, George, 49
Smith, William, 19
Spitz, Arnold, 26
Spitz, Mark, 9, 23, 24, 25–31, 33, 38,
   39, 41
Sohl, Robert, 19
Stack, Allen, 19
Taris, Jean, 15
Tsurata, Yoshujuki, 17
Vendeweghe, Albert, 19
Verdeur, Joseph, 19
Webb, Matthew, 10
Weismuller, Johnny, 12–14, 15, 17,
   22
Wenden, Michael, 30
Wolf, Wallace, 20
Yokoyama, Takahi, 15
Yorzyk, William, 20
Zurner, Albert, 49

PICTURE CREDITS: AP/Wide World Photos, 6, 11, 13, 23, 24, 28, 29, 35, 39, 41, 44, 47, 49, 51, 52, 56, 58; Archive Photos, 15; Archive Photos/A.F.P., 32; Archive Photos, Popperfoto, 16, 18, 37, 61; Reuters/Enrique Shore/Archive Photos, 43; Frontispiece illustration by Steven H. Stroud, 2.

PAULA EDELSON is a freelance writer and journalist. She lives with her husband and two sons in Durham, North Carolina, and is the author of *Male Tennis Stars*, published by Chelsea House Publishers.